WET KISSES

For lovers of Life, Laughter and Love

by
David C Hannibal

Grosvenor House
Publishing Limited

All rights reserved
Copyright © David C Hannibal, 2021

The right of David C Hannibal to be identified as the author of this
work has been asserted in accordance with Section 78
of the Copyright, Designs and Patents Act 1988

The book cover is copyright to David C Hannibal

This book is published by
Grosvenor House Publishing Ltd
Link House
140 The Broadway, Tolworth, Surrey, KT6 7HT.
www.grosvenorhousepublishing.co.uk

This book is sold subject to the conditions that it shall not, by way of
trade or otherwise, be lent, resold, hired out or otherwise circulated
without the author's or publisher's prior consent in any form of binding or
cover other than that in which it is published and
without a similar condition including this condition being imposed
on the subsequent purchaser.

This book is a work of fiction. Any resemblance to
people or events, past or present, is purely coincidental.

A CIP record for this book
is available from the British Library

ISBN 978-1-83975-476-0

For Rita and Maria

It was always just the three of us

This is a collection of work in distinct sections.

To say that words are important, is a classic case of stating the blindingly obvious. Without words, how can we possibly articulate feelings of love, affection and humour, as expressed by troubadours throughout the ages in poem, song, love-letter and storytelling?

This contribution is my tribute to all those words of love that have been spoken and listened to for as long as there has been civilisation ... and lovers.

I hope you enjoy them.

CONTENTS

An introduction to the meaning of love   1

A selection of poems, a short story, and a love song without music.

What is Love?	3
Love	4
Valentine	5
Wet Kissing	6
Kissing	7
Who am I?	9
A love song without music	17

Love Poems   19

An array of 36 poems designed to bring joy to the most jaded of souls. Poetry touching on boundless determination of love lost and found. With provocative thoughts of love – or its very notion – you must decide.

Poems of reflection   57

Discover 12 poems which touch on the deeper aspects of the ephemeral nature of life.

Humorous poems   71

21 poems to scratch the surface of what makes us laugh - from the sublime to the ridiculous.

Poem of uncertainty   95

A poem to question reality.

The big Finish   99

A pithy analysis of the circle of life

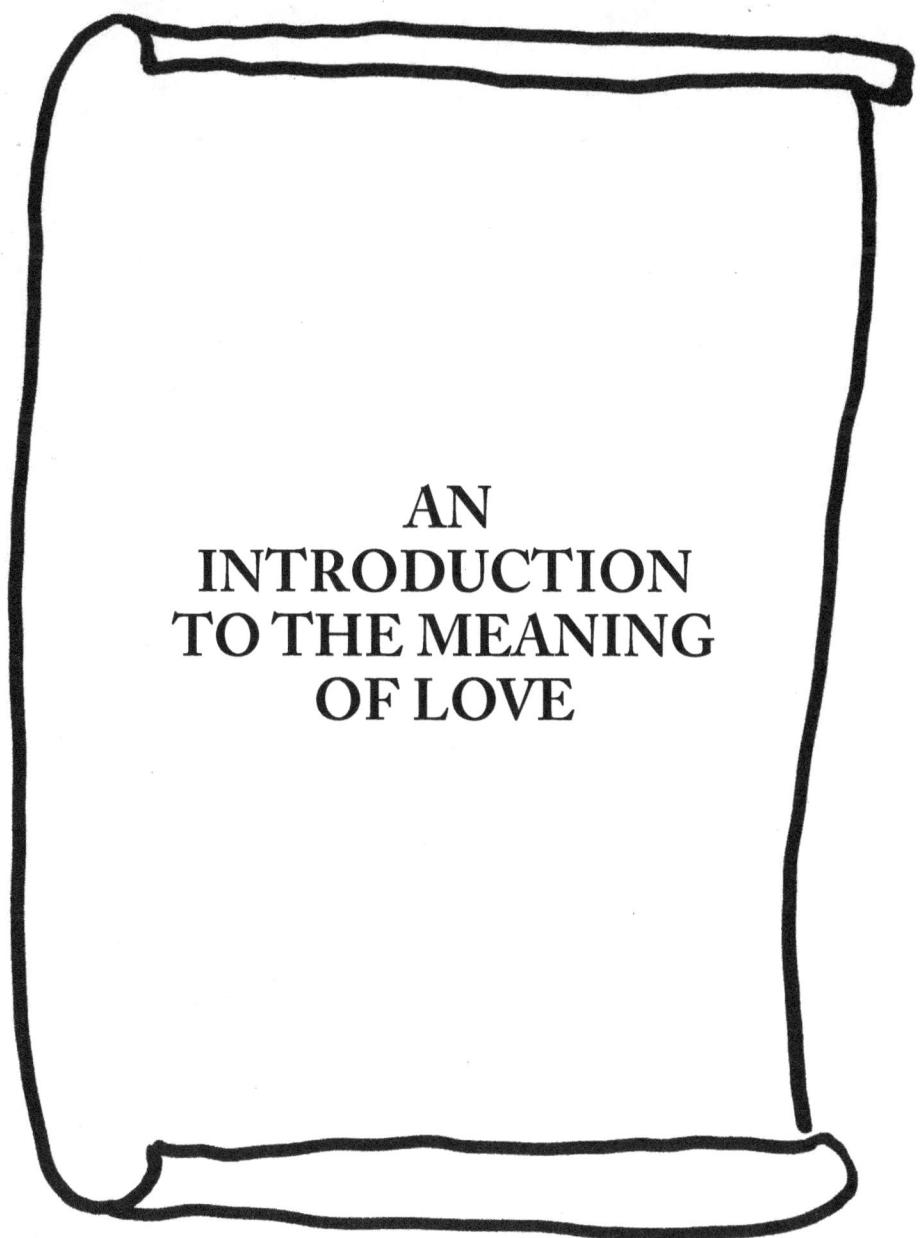

AN INTRODUCTION TO THE MEANING OF LOVE

WHAT IS LOVE?

What is love? It is a masquerade
That every child has played
Under a summer sun

What is love? It is a game for two
A game for me and you
A game that's just begun

What is love? It is a story told
Between the young and old
About the way it's done

What is love? A magic tapestry
Between the sun and sea
Enjoyed by everyone

Now I see the many things I missed before
Now I see the mystery behind the door
Now I see you're all I need and what is more
Now I see it's only you I'm living for
Now I see
Now I see
Now I see

LOVE

It can make you laugh
It can make you cry
It can make you scream
It can make you sigh
Not entirely safe
Like a fairground ride
Better hold on tight
And enjoy the ride

VALENTINE

Will the journey of life for me and you
Be one double ticket
Or a single for two
If you look in your heart you'll see a sign
Will you make me complete
And be my Valentine

WET KISSING

The wetter the kiss
The better the bliss

KISSING

Kissing me gently
And kissing me well
Will take me places
Only Angels dwell

A SHORT STORY

WHO AM I?

I woke up this morning and found myself lying on a bed, looking into the face of a sleeping woman I didn't recognise. As she lay there, my thoughts became more confused. Who was she? What was she doing here? Come to that, what was *I* doing here?

Looking around, it was obvious that my surroundings were just as unfamiliar to me. It was a rather smart looking hotel suite that would be way beyond the likes of, say a housewife or travelling salesman, but very popular with business executives or classy working girls. I looked again at the woman sleeping in the bed, she was a real beauty, but she didn't look much like a business executives, surely she couldn't be ....?

As I struggled with my memory, the struggle quickly turned to panic, as the more I tried to think, the less I seemed to be able to remember.

Quietly I got out of bed and moved to the bathroom. I was in a daze, even as I showered my thoughts still in turmoil. I had a strange sense of impending doom, guilt even, but for the life of me I couldn't think why.

Suddenly, my mind was filled with a single image that hit me like a bolt of lightning. A haggard face was looking at me through the mist of the bathroom. As I looked closer, I realised that the haggard face looking back at me was a reflection from the bathroom mirror. It was even worse than I had thought, not only did I not recognise the woman in the bed, I didn't recognise myself either.

My state of shock was suddenly interrupted by the sound of a fierce struggle coming from the bedroom. Before I could gather my senses, the bathroom door burst open, and a hooded figure rushed in. I was aware of the smell of chloroform, then, very slowly, all the lights went out. I woke up cold and shivering on the bathroom floor, and staggered shakily into the bedroom. It was really no surprise to me, to find the room was empty. Realising I was still naked, as quickly as I could I dressed and then sat down to try and put together all the events of the last few minutes. Minutes? My goodness it seemed like hours, but I had to try and clear my mind, think rationally, be logical. It wasn't going to be easy, but I knew what had to be done. Slowly but surely, I felt a calmness and determination sweep over me. Although I didn't know what I was going to find out, about what had happened, about the girl or about me, I only knew that if it was the last thing I did, I *would* find out.

Despite a throbbing headache, my eyes suddenly focused on a note by the bed. It was hastily written in a childish scrawl, but the contents were anything *but* childish. It read 'bring £10,000 by tonight if you want her back, and don't tell the police'. Panic began to sweep over me once more. Who was the girl and why on earth would I want her back? where did I have to take the money? Why couldn't I tell the police? What had happened? And more to the point, where was I supposed to get that sort of money from anyway?

I could see there was no luggage in the room, so I emptied my pockets, and took stock of my meagre personal possessions looking for something, anything to help me. There were some keys, a final demand gas bill, credit cards and a cheque book. It wasn't much, but it was a start.

There was an address on the gas bill - Flat 2, 18 Bakery Avenue, so I thought that was as good a starting point as any. However, in my panic, I rushed out of the hotel without looking properly and stupidly knocked into a young woman, pushing her against a parked car she had been admiring, a gleaming Rolls Royce as it happened. Just my luck I thought, not just a young woman, but a young policewoman who turned and gave me a cool look. 'Someone's in a mad hurry' she said 'what's the problem?' On the spur of the moment I said 'I'm so sorry, but it's my boss's gas, I'm in a hurry to stop them cutting him off' and showed her the bill. Then she smiled and said 'that's alright, it's not often I'm nearly pushed into a Rolls Royce, but take it easy now, no harm done'. All I could think of at that moment were the words on the note 'don't tell the police', but at least I had the presence of mind, and after saying 'I wouldn't mind a car like that myself', to ask for directions to Bakery Street. She said it was only a ten minute walk away. I made it in two, and sure enough, after knocking and getting no reply, found that one of my keys fitted the lock, and I went in. There was quite a collection of mail behind the front door, and from the look of it, no one had been there for a while. The letters were all addressed to Simon Morley, the same name that was on the cheque book and credit cards. I thought I might as well sign that name on the back of an envelope, and sure enough it matched the signature on the credit cards. At least I'd now discovered who *I* was, so all I had to do was figure out *what* I was, who *she* was, how I could get £10,000 and what I was going to do next.

The flat was tatty, and a quick look around confirmed that I obviously lived there alone. The clothes in the wardrobe were quite smart, but nothing in the flat seemed to give any clues as to what I might have been, or what I might have done for a living. I picked up a recent copy of a local newspaper bearing the headline 'Daring security firm robbery nets lone villain over half a million pounds' and began to sort automatically through the bundle of letters. I was disturbed from this task by a knock on the front door. After a pause, I opened it and was confronted by a little old lady who started speaking rapidly. My head was still a little thick, and I tried to concentrate on what she was saying, but heard only random phrases 'Mrs Moore' - 'next door neighbour' – 'trouble' - 'police'. My mind froze as I heard her mention police. Still clutching the newspaper and wad of mail, I rushed past the startled old lady, slamming the door behind me. I walked quickly away from the flat, back towards the hotel. With my mind working furiously, I stepped into the welcoming quiet of a discreet wine bar, and at a corner table began to once more collect my thoughts.

Taking a deep breath, I began to sort through the mail I was carrying, and, after discarding the usual junk mail, was left with three envelopes and a folded note. For some reason I put the folded note straight into my pocket without reading it, and opened the first envelope. I read the contents six or seven times before I accepted that it was a vehicle registration document. It appeared genuine, and was no big deal really, apart from the fact that the brand new vehicle, now registered in my name, was a Rolls Royce.

Determined to see if it was a coincidence or not, I made my way back to the hotel, making sure I wasn't being followed. Sure enough, the Rolls Royce the policewoman had been admiring outside the hotel was the one registered in my name. One of my keys duly opened the car door and I sat behind the wheel, for a brief moment feeling that the world was my oyster, before coming to the conclusion that it was probably a very good idea to get as far away from the hotel as quickly as I could. I drove north for an hour or so feeling like a prince, before finally parking in a quiet cul-de-sac to decide my next move.

Somehow I felt that I had some vital pieces of the puzzle, although I still lacked the ability to put them together. As I reached into my pocket for the remaining letters, the first thing that came to hand was the folded note. It was written in the same childish scrawl as the first note, and said 'we aim to get to you before the police do, and remember, you said you'd share some of the money with us. Call Martyn now at the phone number below, if you want to stop us making a mess of Angela'. Angela, so that was the name of the beauty at the hotel, and at long last, here was a phone number, a point of contact, now I was getting somewhere. I opened the next envelope; it was a bank statement, showing a credit balance on my account of £538,199.75. I stared for what seemed an age at the balance, £538,199.75. Then my eyes went to the newspaper, with the headline, 'Daring security firm robbery nets lone villain over half a million pounds'. Although I still couldn't remember anything of the past, it seemed clear to me now that I was a wanted man, and had a great deal to answer for. The next letter was already open. It was the hotel booking confirmation for me and Angela, well that explained how the kidnappers found me. At least now I knew I had the money, all I had to do was take a chance, go to my bank, and hope the police hadn't got on my trail yet. I realised that Angela was suddenly very important to me, and I'd better do as they say and finish this thing.

I was apprehensive about getting the money from the bank, but in the end there was no trouble at all. Next I had to call this Martyn at the phone number on the note. I was told to go to a disused wing at the local hospital at 8pm where if I did as I was told, Angela would not be messed up. Soon, everything would be over. I had the money. I knew what I had to do to get Angela back. I had enough money to be able to stay one step ahead of the police. We could make a new life abroad. If only we could get through tonight.

After driving around for a few hours, it was finally time to make my way to my rendezvous with Martyn. There was just a couple of miles to go when I hit a traffic jam. I could see ahead to the two cars that were blocking the road, and could also see a police car coming out from a side street to deal with the incident. I let it go in front of me, and saw that in the passenger seat of the police car, was the young policewoman I had seen earlier outside the hotel. I tried to look away, but she got a good look at me as the car went by.

I quickly turned down the side road and made a few more left and rights, before finally abandoning my car in a dimly lit street. I didn't know exactly where I was, but knew I was only about 30 minutes away from the meeting place with Martyn, and I could still just about make it on time. I took my briefcase containing the money, and, ignoring the police sirens, ducked into the welcoming shadows, and continued on foot. Finally, I arrived at the disused wing of the hospital, and in my mind, went over the other instructions I'd been given, which were, go to the second floor, turn right, second corridor turn left, fourth door on the right, room number 13. Suddenly I heard a distant clock chiming, and realised that it was already 8 o'clock.

Rushing wildly up the stairs, I found room 13 and paused to catch my breath. I saw a light under the doors and heard noises coming from inside. My stomach was in knots as I tensed myself to go in. Just as I reached for the door handle I heard another door slam along the corridor, and saw the silhouette of a police helmet.

I felt my world fall apart, but consoled myself in the knowledge that even if my plans were in ruins, at least Angela would soon be free.

I went through the door, and was met by a bizarre sight, so bizarre that for what seemed like an eternity, I couldn't speak. Angela was tied to a bed, and there were three men in white coats standing around her, saying 'you're late' and taking it in turns to pour custard on her hair. I was vaguely aware that a policeman had put his hand on my shoulder, at the same moment that a brilliant white light exploded in my brain. As the brilliant light slowly faded, my memory came flooding back. I knew who I was, who Angela was, what the idiots in white coats were doing, as well as who the policeman was. The room became full of laughter and back slapping as I blurted out my story.

Angela and I were in fact newlyweds, having married only a couple of days ago in a registry office. We were spending the night at a nearby hotel before meeting Angela's parents to take them on the holiday of a lifetime. I had been worried about how they would react about not waiting for a church wedding, but, following a big win on the football pools, we decided not to wait. That, and the fact that Angela's shift pattern as a nurse in a children's ward meant she could suddenly take a couple of weeks off. Angela was getting 'messed up' as part of the medical student's rag week, and she had also got some of her young patients to join in the fun, by writing the various notes in the stunt. If my memory had not been lost I would have remembered that the £10,000 was the amount I'd promised to give to the hospital following my pools win, and the reference about telling the police, stemmed from the fact that Angela's father was a policeman. The very one who had just put his hand on my shoulder as I walked in the room. He'd been busy on the big robbery case, and was coming to leave word for Angela that the robber had been arrested following a routine traffic accident, and that our holiday could go ahead as planned. Dr Martyn Moore, who had been the 'contact' I had telephoned, and was still busy pouring custard over Angela's head, thought I had sounded a little weird on the telephone, but had put it down to the liberal use of chloroform during the 'kidnapping'.

At which point I made a mental note to take a bunch of flowers to his mother, a little old lady neighbour, who probably thinks my behaviour was pretty strange, even for an ex travelling salesman.

And my memory? well all I can say is, that's the last time I volunteer from the audience, for 'The Great Bertini', master hypnotist. Angela thought I'd been marvellous up on stage. She never suspected that I was still 'under the influence' when we got back to the hotel. 'The Great Bertini' had said that only the very stupid stayed 'under the influence' for more than five minutes , but as I looked at my beautiful Angela, and remembered my bank balance, I thought 'how can I be called stupid?'. Now, if only I could remember where I left my Rolls Royce..........................

A love song without music - create your own

What's going on					Verse
Another day is done
A day that saw me drifting and where nothing much mattered
No time to run
Are all my dreams intact
Or are they blown away and on the winds of time scattered

There's got to be another way				Chorus
But fools die as they're learning
Can wisdom wait another day
The world is gently burning

I see the light					Verse
At least I think I do
But I don't know for certain if mankind is here to stay
I'd like to know
Just for my peace of mind
If someone knows the answer do you think that they might say

Repeat Chorus

Can dreamers see					Verse
Another way of life
Pity anybody not believing in a poet
He may just be
The solitary key
Having all the answers, but it's up to you to know it

Repeat Chorus

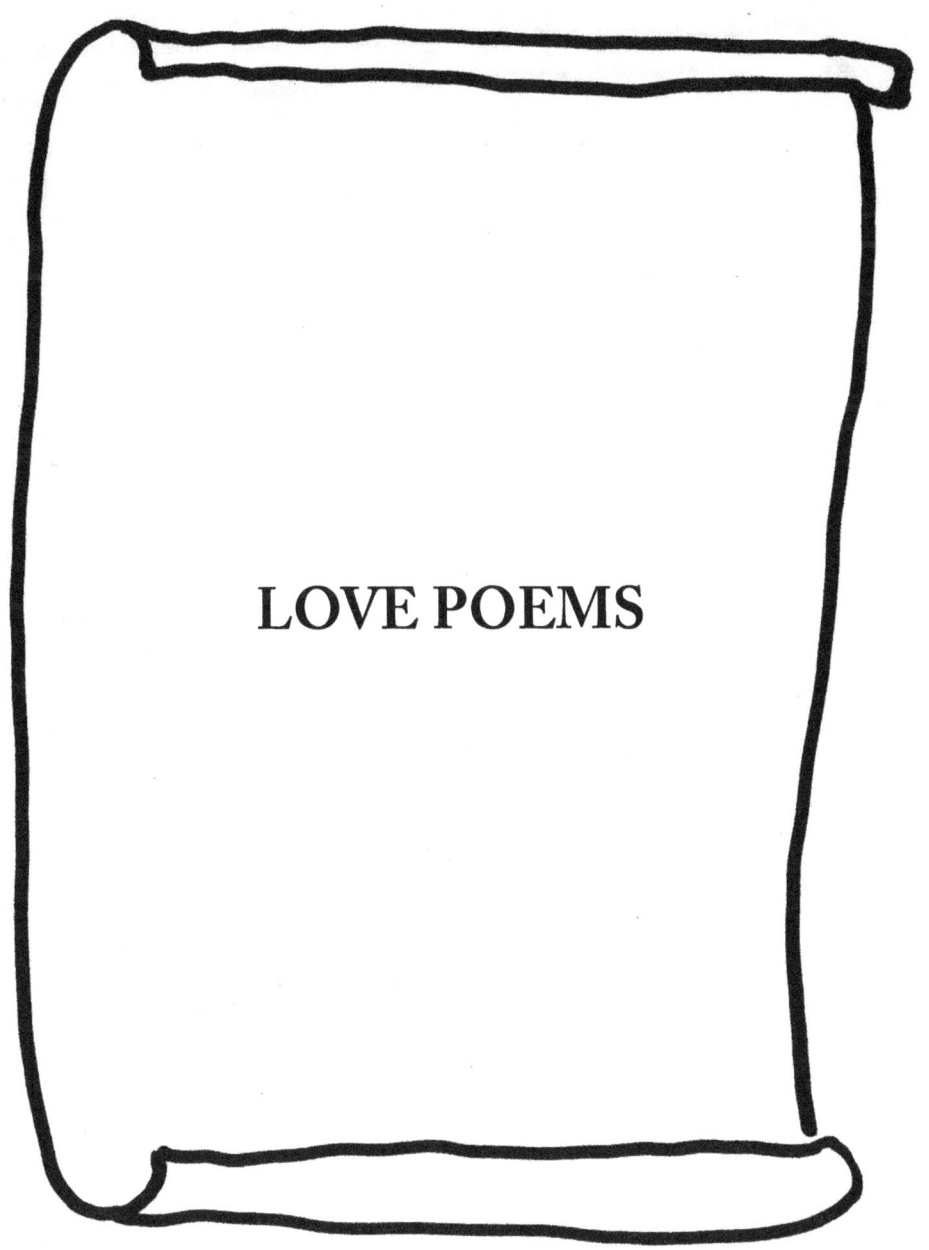
LOVE POEMS

1

You are my rainbow
You bring me colours
In a grey world you paint my sky
And though I've known you
For just a short time
I will love you until I die

2

Believe in what you're holding
And in what is holding you
Let sunrise be the signal
To begin what you must do

3

Remember all the thrills we knew
When first we met before love grew
Before our lifelines were entwined
Now I can see where I was blind

4

She spoke to me without a word
But if she had would I have heard
As clearly as I had those eyes
That promised me such paradise

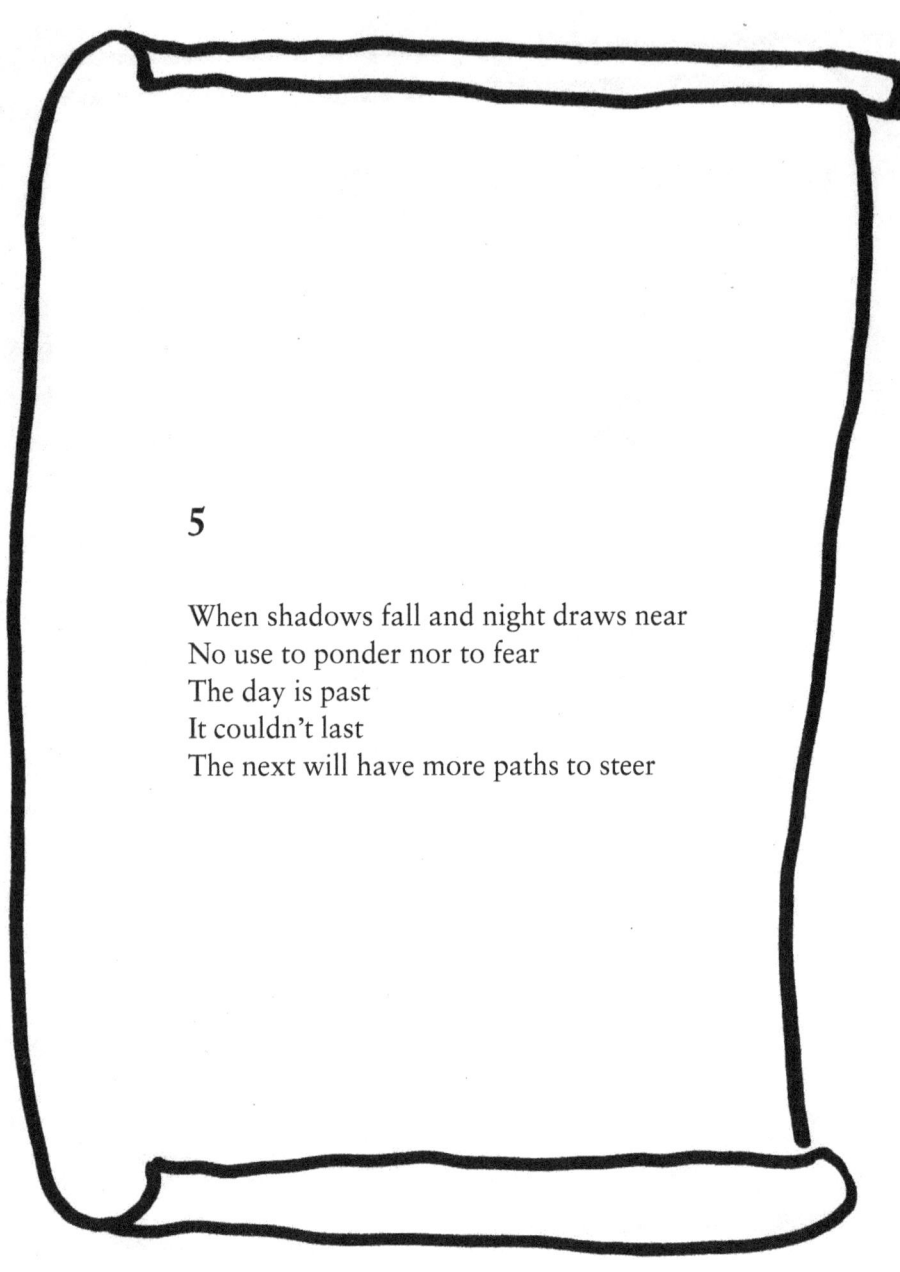

5

When shadows fall and night draws near
No use to ponder nor to fear
The day is past
It couldn't last
The next will have more paths to steer

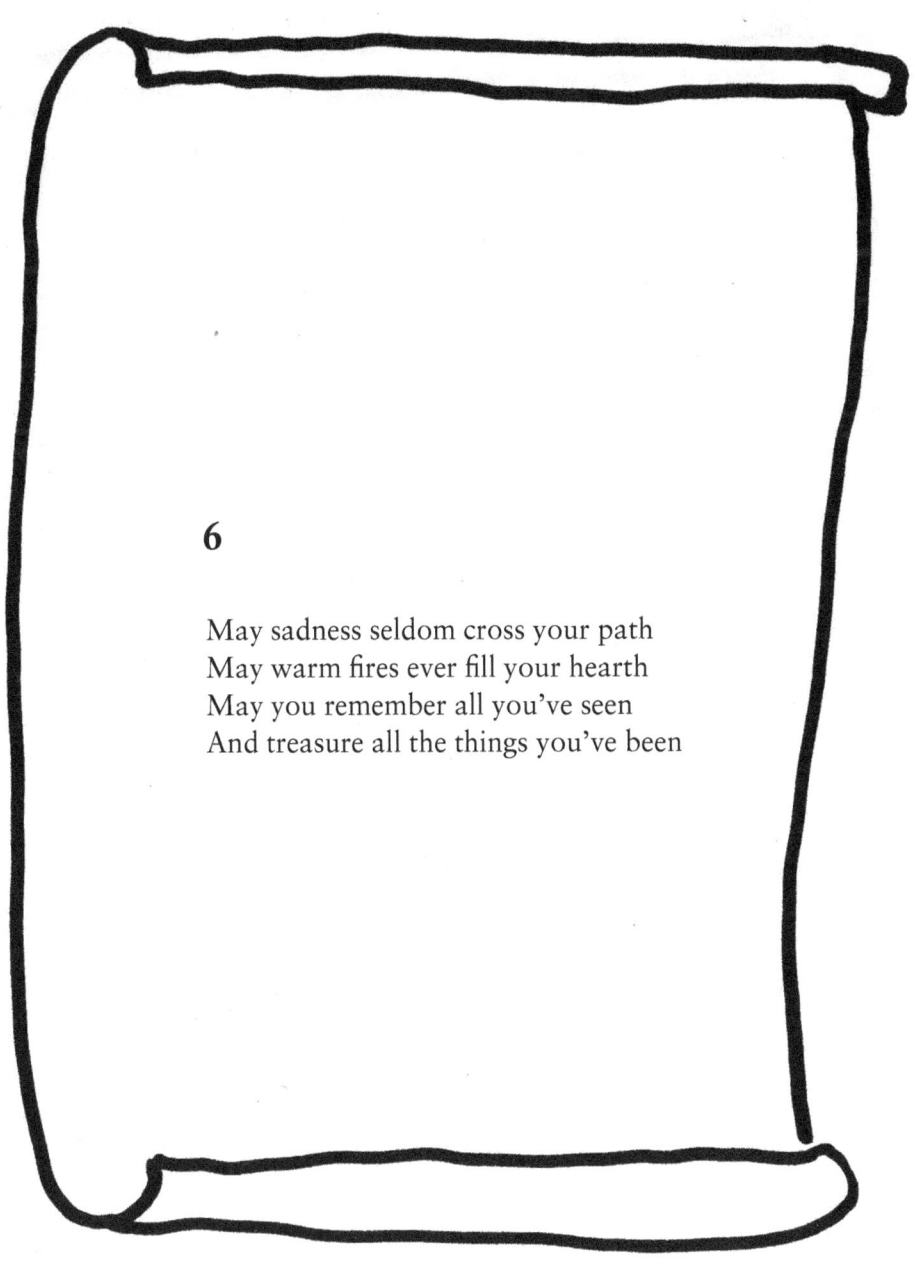

6

May sadness seldom cross your path
May warm fires ever fill your hearth
May you remember all you've seen
And treasure all the things you've been

7

Too soon the day we understand
That we are all just grains of sand
And everything we ever planned
Becomes a simple memory

And all the things that we hold dear
In focus now so crystal clear
Will very shortly disappear
And merely be a used to be

8

There's more to life than kiss and run
Or looking in a bottle for the way it's done

There's more to life than kiss and tell
Or throwing all your money in a wishing well

9

I just want to hold you close
Kiss your cheek, feel we are one
Let me look into your eyes
Cast a spell, there – it is done

10

So many things still to be said
So much still to be done
May peaceful ways and sunny days
Fill all the years to come

11

May you know the true meaning of happiness
May you understand all that you see
May you always know where you are going, and
Be the person that you want to be

12

Will I be in your memory
Will I be in your heart
Will I be at your journeys end
As I am at the start

13

Destination - who can tell
And the future – who can say
'Till you get to know me well
We should live from day to day

Think of me as one who knows
Where I always want to be
As to where destiny blows
Stick around and you will see

14

A tear drop glistened in her eye
As hurriedly she passed me by
I wished to understand her so
But like a fool I let her go
Regretting what I could not ask
Without the words for such a task

15

Vision dressed in satin and lace
With tender eyes and smiling face
A whisper like a soft caress
Epitome of happiness

16

I could not do what I do without you
My inspiration and my sanity
I could not be what I am without you
And I thank God that you are here with me

17

In you I have everything I need
I will gladly follow where you lead
How lucky I am that you desire me
That very knowledge does so inspire me

18

If there is anything that I
Could hold more precious than your love
I doubt that it is of this world
Unless it fell from Heav'n above

19

I'll always think of you as laughter in the rain
Someone who gave me hope and love time and again
Who gave me only happiness and kissed away the pain
I'll always think of you my love as laughter in the rain

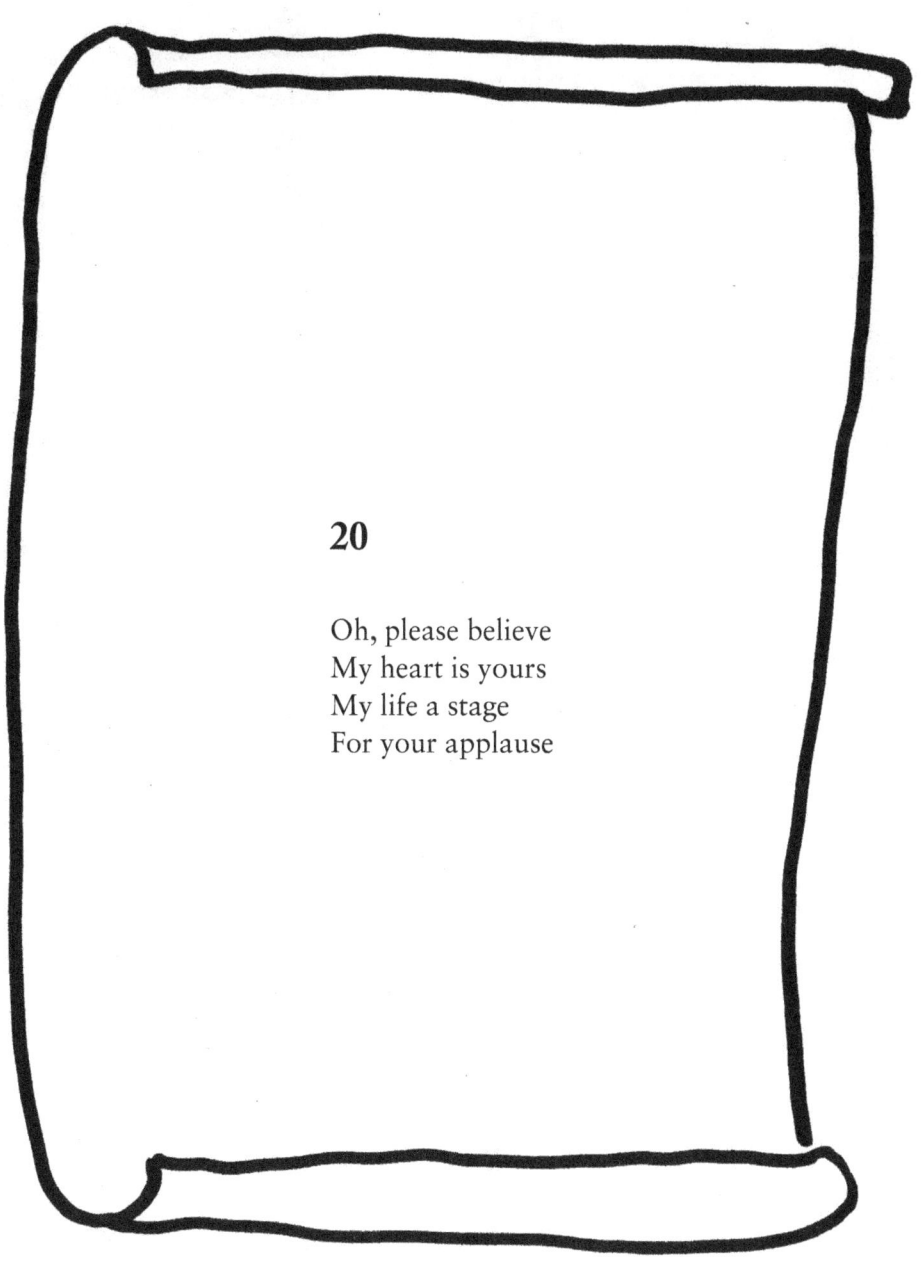

20

Oh, please believe
My heart is yours
My life a stage
For your applause

21

THINK OF ME
When a gentle breeze touches your face
As my own hands once had done
And the warmth of our embrace is felt
As the heat from summer sun

And when rain is falling down your cheeks
Like the tears together cried
When the sheer delight of our loving
Could no longer be denied
THINK OF ME

22

Life is our garden
Hope is our seed
Promise our harvest
Doubts are a weed
Dreams are our water
Care is a shoot
Patience our future
Love is our fruit

23

Be a part of what I'm doing
Be a part of who I am
You can show me you're a woman
As I show you I'm a man

Watch me now and I'll try to help
For it isn't hard to do
Just come and get up close to me
While I get up close to you

24

If I could only help you see
All of the things that we could be
If I could hold you close to me
You'd see our love would set us free

25

Will it make you sigh, will it make you shout
Will it chew you up, will it spit you out

Will the love you need ever burn the same
As some gasoline and a naked flame

Will a love endure on a lonely road
Will it fill your heart only to explode

Will it make you sing, will it make you roar?
Will you cry enough, will you beg for more?

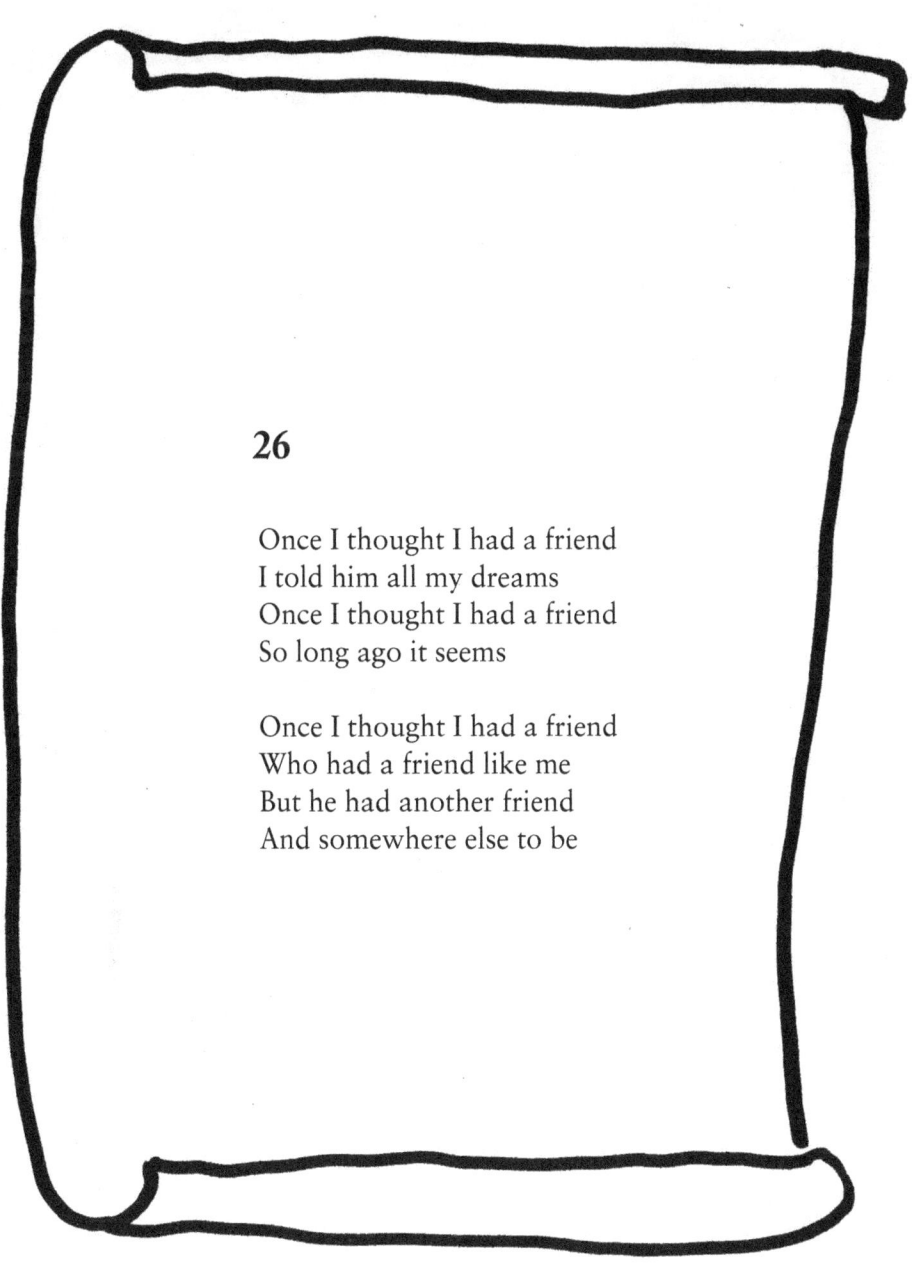

26

Once I thought I had a friend
I told him all my dreams
Once I thought I had a friend
So long ago it seems

Once I thought I had a friend
Who had a friend like me
But he had another friend
And somewhere else to be

27

Your lips and arms I'll borrow
But I'll give them back in time
Enough I had them for a while
And once could call them mine

28

Have you got the time to know me
Learn my secrets and to show me
How I need your contribution
To my problem and solution

29

Maybe nothing really matters
Maybe nothing here is real
So just hang on to your vision
And to what it is you feel

30

Love, unlike the season
Begins with no reason
And ends in the very same way
Nothing lasts forever
But if you are clever
You keep it for more than a day

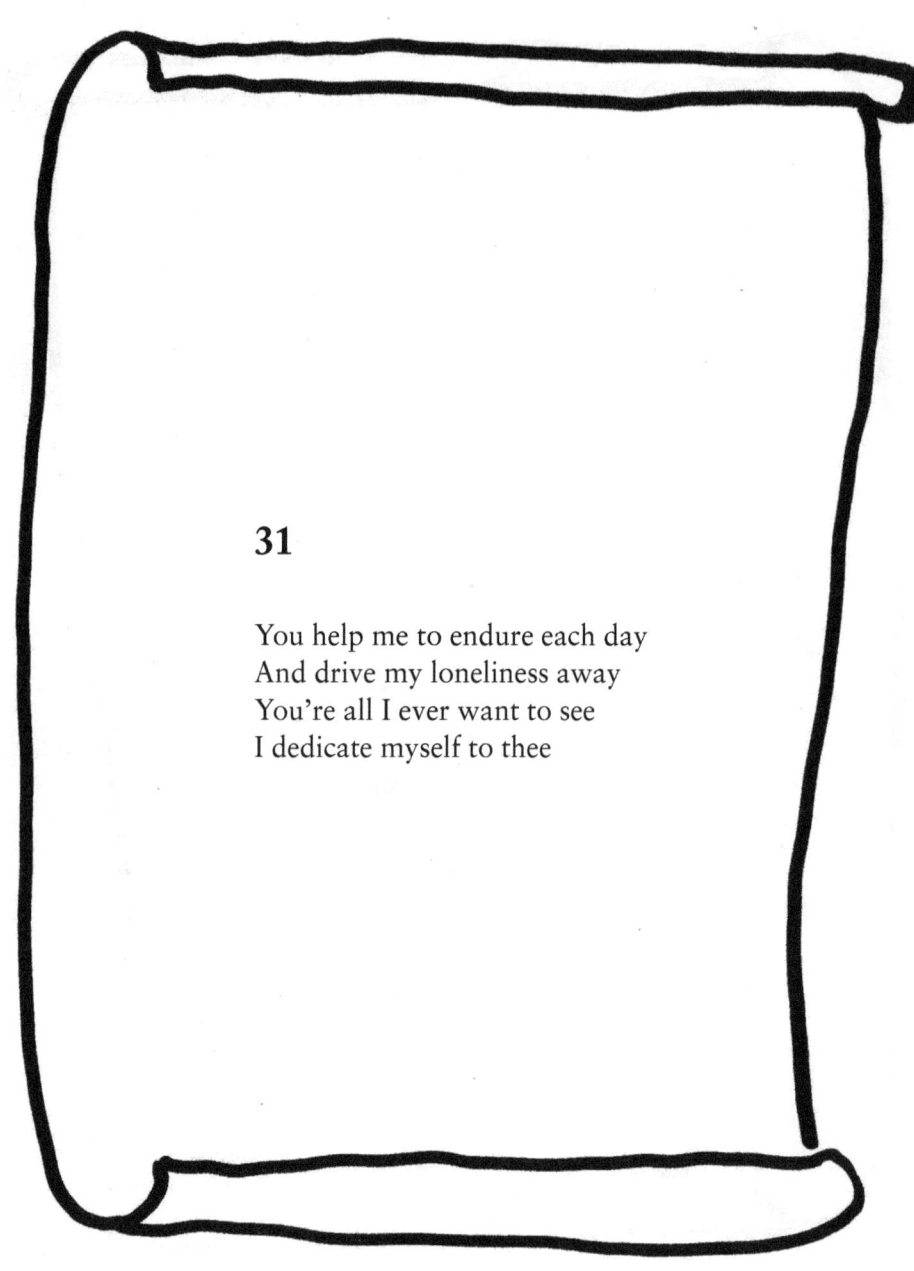

31

You help me to endure each day
And drive my loneliness away
You're all I ever want to see
I dedicate myself to thee

32

In my pursuit of happiness
I found a dream I might possess
To you, the dream I so adore
I pledge my love for evermore

33

Such words go round inside my head
About my love for you
My heart is fit to burst with pride
About all that you do

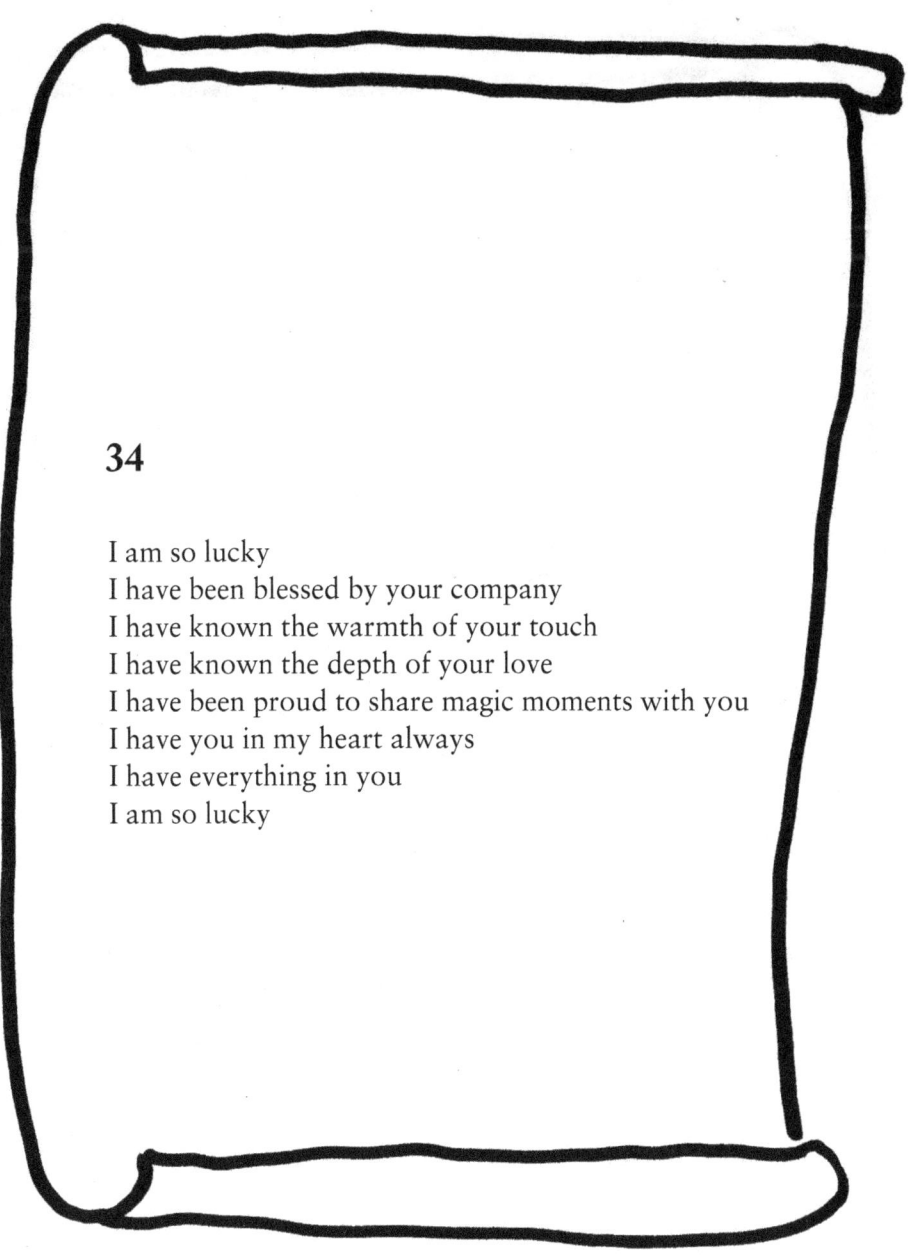

34

I am so lucky
I have been blessed by your company
I have known the warmth of your touch
I have known the depth of your love
I have been proud to share magic moments with you
I have you in my heart always
I have everything in you
I am so lucky

35

When the lord of all you hate
Is coming at you from the past
When the things you left behind
Begin to catch up with you fast
When you share your dream and find
That no one wants your dream to last
That's the time I recommend
You nail your colours to the mast

And make your stand even though
Nobody's there to take your hand
Just stand your ground even though
There's not another soul around
There are times for changing course
And times to back another horse
But when your runnings over
Then that's the time you make your stand

When you feel the way ahead
Is oh so rocky and so vast
And the things you had to do
No longer seem to be a blast
And when someone tries to say
It's over, and the die is cast
That's the time I recommend
You nail your colours to the mast

When you're crying fit to burst
But no one round you hears your voice
When they tell you what to do
And never once give you a choice
When your backs against the wall
And if they say that you're outclassed
That's the time I recommend
You nail your colours to the mast

36

Thanks for sharing all you have with me
Thanks for giving me the chance to see
That a new day always greets the morning sun
And by loving you my life has just begun

Thanks for sharing in my destiny
Thanks for simply being here with me
I can sense there is a battle to be won
And by loving you my life has just begun

POEMS OF REFLECTION

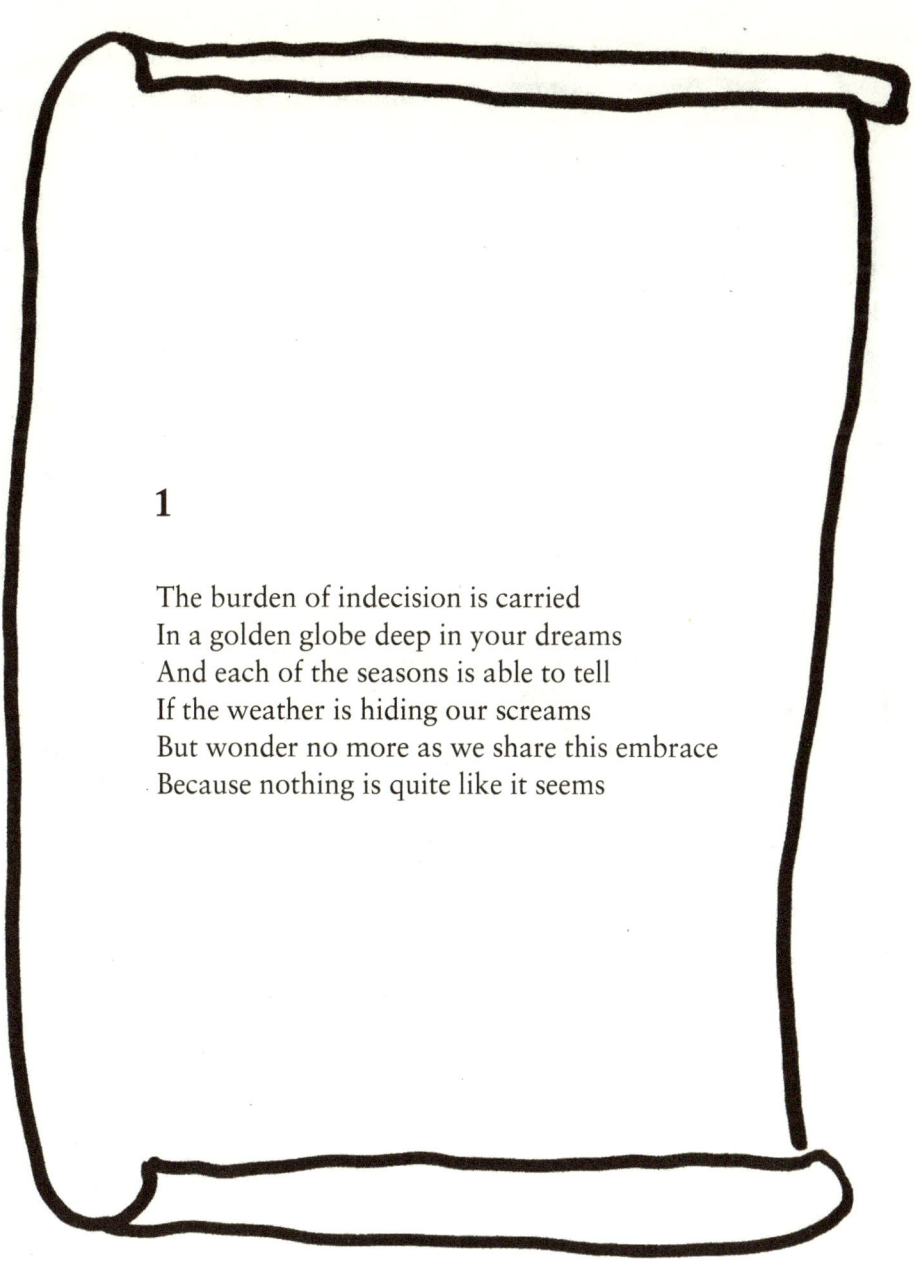

1

The burden of indecision is carried
In a golden globe deep in your dreams
And each of the seasons is able to tell
If the weather is hiding our screams
But wonder no more as we share this embrace
Because nothing is quite like it seems

2

Tell the wind you're only bending not breaking
Tell the clouds you're not so frightened of the rain
And tell whoever listens
They will never, ever win
Knock me down and I'll just get right up again

3

Don't ask me 'bout tomorrow
Just remember yesterday
Don't ask me if I understand
The things you try to say

Don't ask me 'bout tomorrow
And of all the things you've planned
Don't ask me if I've lost a dream
Like water into sand

4

I've had my fill
Of foolish thrills
That never seem to last

The silly days
And careless ways
Of going nowhere fast

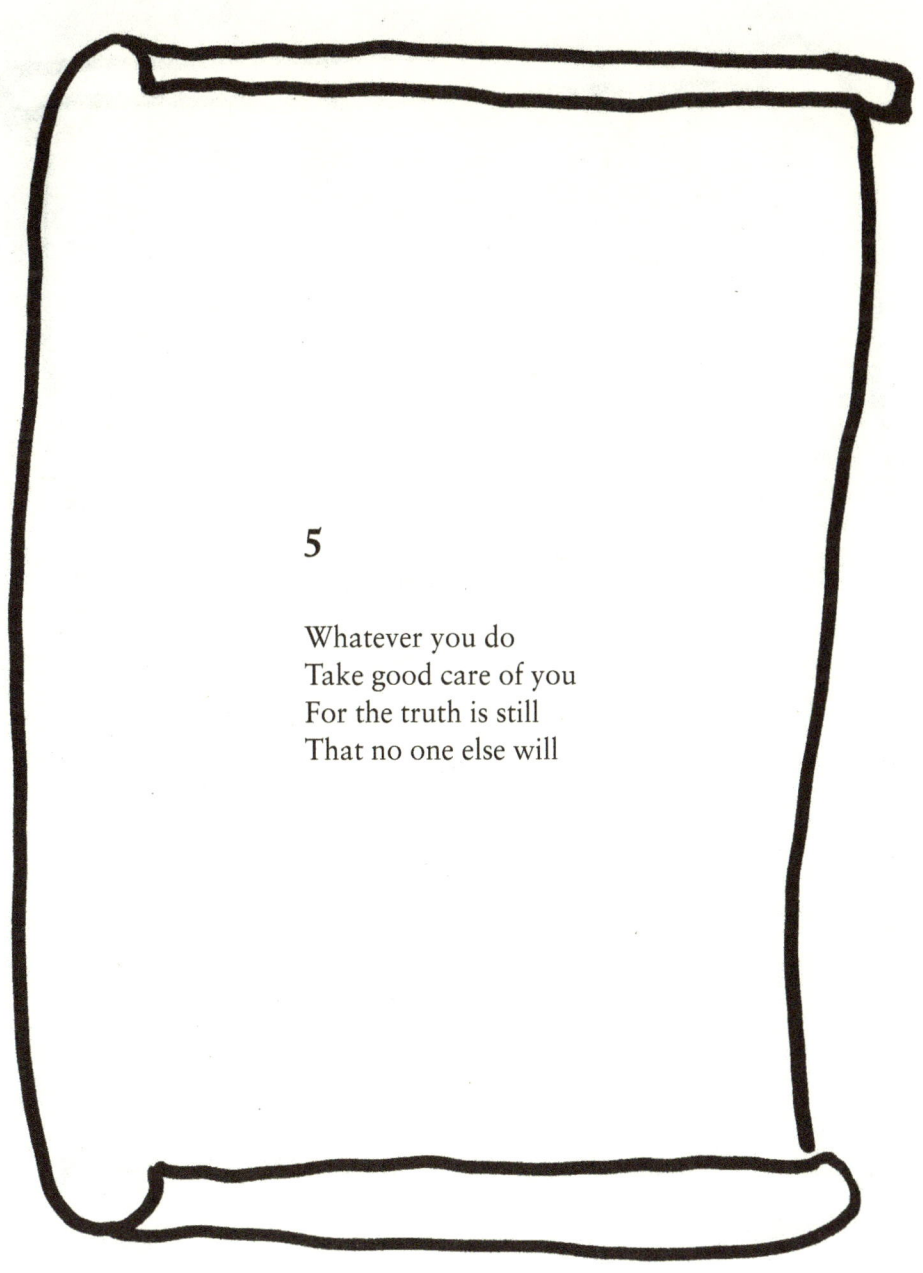

5

Whatever you do
Take good care of you
For the truth is still
That no one else will

6

There's a wrinkle or two
And a bulge here and there
And there isn't as much
Of that thick greasy hair

Now the eyes start to squint
When you're trying to read
And those little old legs
Don't have quite so much speed

Now your hand starts to shake
When you're signing your name
And threading a needle
Is a very long game

But now face up to facts
You must surely agree
You've been feeling like this
Since you turned twenty three

7

Give me one more kiss before you go
One more kiss I will remember
Hold me tightly one last time
Then if you must just walk away

8

Where would the climber be without any rope
Where would the cleaner be without any soap
Where would the old frog be without any spawn
Where would the old stag be without any fawn
Where would the priest be without any cloisters
Where would the pearl be without any oysters
Where would the farmer be without any land
Where would the Arab be without any sand
Where would wallpaper be without any glue
Where on earth would I be without any you

9

I can see the far horizon
Hear the wind call out my name
I must travel to tomorrow
Or my soul must take the blame

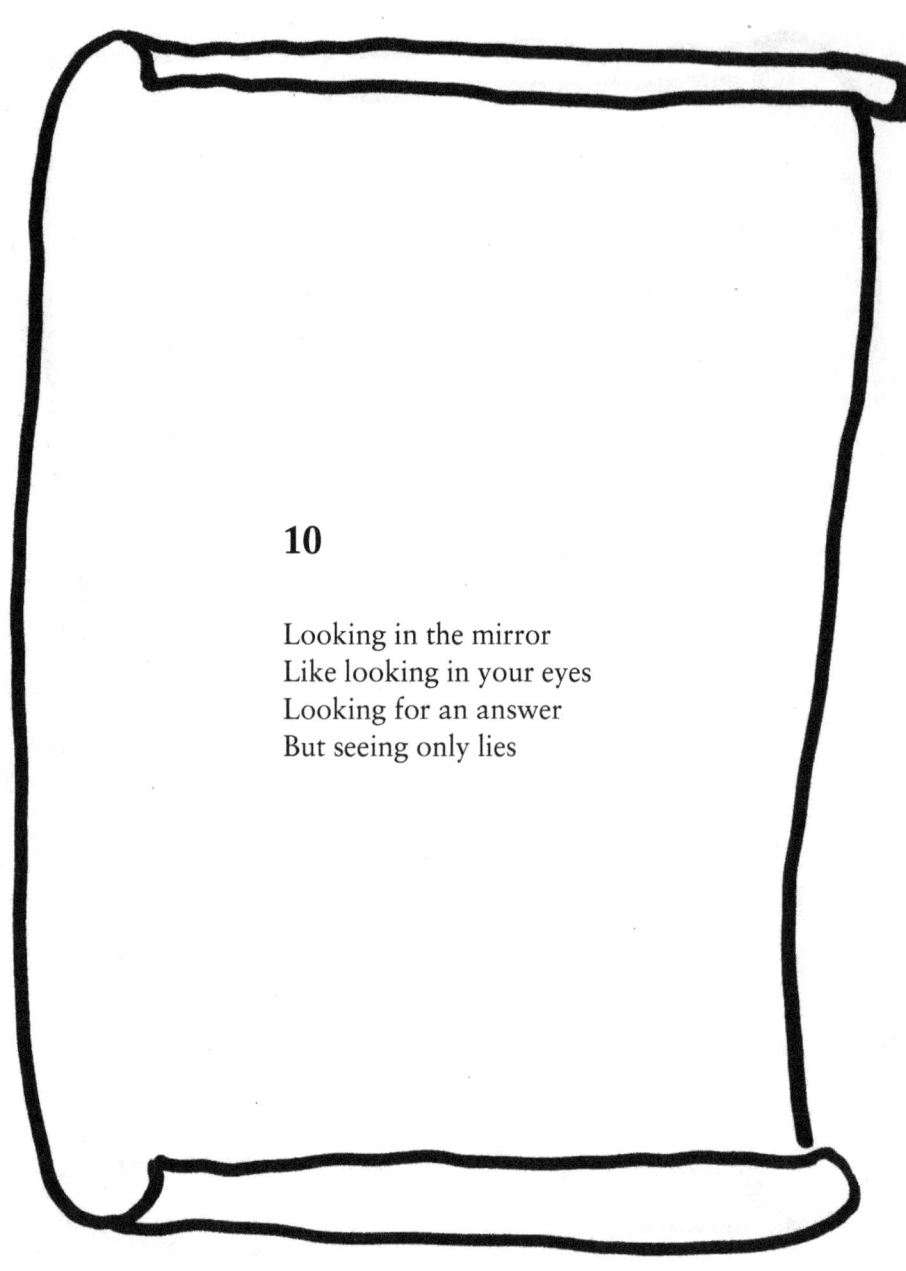

10

Looking in the mirror
Like looking in your eyes
Looking for an answer
But seeing only lies

11

Just as if a castle
Was swallowed by the sand
Yesterday's tomorrow
Is not the way I planned

12

I watch the falling grains of sand
That slowly leave the reapers hand
I cannot tear my eyes away
And gently goes another day

This fatal fascination goes
When reason through the torment shows
To light the path where I must tread
To concentrate on life instead

In future I must look right through
And see the things that I must do
For losers are the ones who stare
And winners those who dare to dare

HUMOROUS POEMS

1

You know I've a hunch that you're gonna go far
Said Mrs Modo to her young son Quasi
Just steer clear of churches, and young girls and bells
But he just wasn't listening, was he

2

I'm going down the doctors
Yes I'm going down the quacks
To pick up me prescription
That'll help me to relax

Me nerves are shot to ribbons
I'm coiled up like a spring
I'm flying round in circles
Like a bird with just one wing

3

When the sweating and grunting and heaving is done
And there's no more discomfort or pain
You can look in the face of the one that you love
And say – let's not have curry again

4a

Ode to a bridegroom

As graduation day draws near
And as both cheeks start to sweat
You recall your stag night stripper
And what you did for a bet

Just think of what a man must do
Like a nine dart 301
A 147 snooker break
Or a three wood hole in one

But all this can seem a doddle
When you're waiting in the aisle
Trying so hard not to break wind
While you're trying hard to smile

Then when you get the chance to speak
You can answer with a laugh
When they ask 'will you take this girl;
Say, you're joking, me? not 'arf

4b

Marriage

The first forty years are real easy
It's the next forty years you need care
For then the memory starts to go
And you're not sure just what goes quite where

5

Will it be alright here with you tonight
Or will it make us a love statistic
Will we stay the course, will we calm the force
Or just crumble away like a biscuit

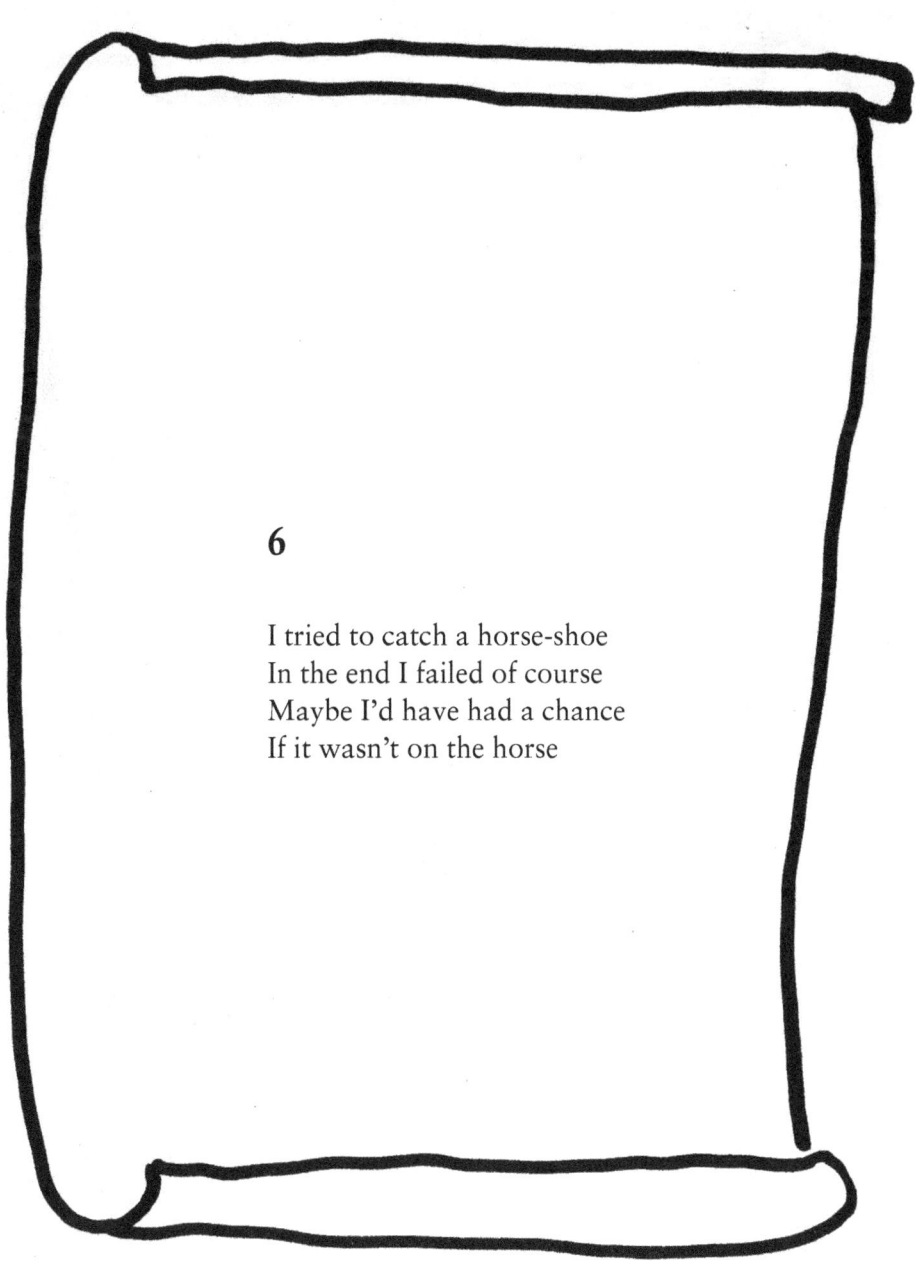

6

I tried to catch a horse-shoe
In the end I failed of course
Maybe I'd have had a chance
If it wasn't on the horse

7

A man had a bee sting on his private parts
So he rushed to the surgery yelling
Oh doctor please take away all of my pain
But I beg you please leave all the swelling

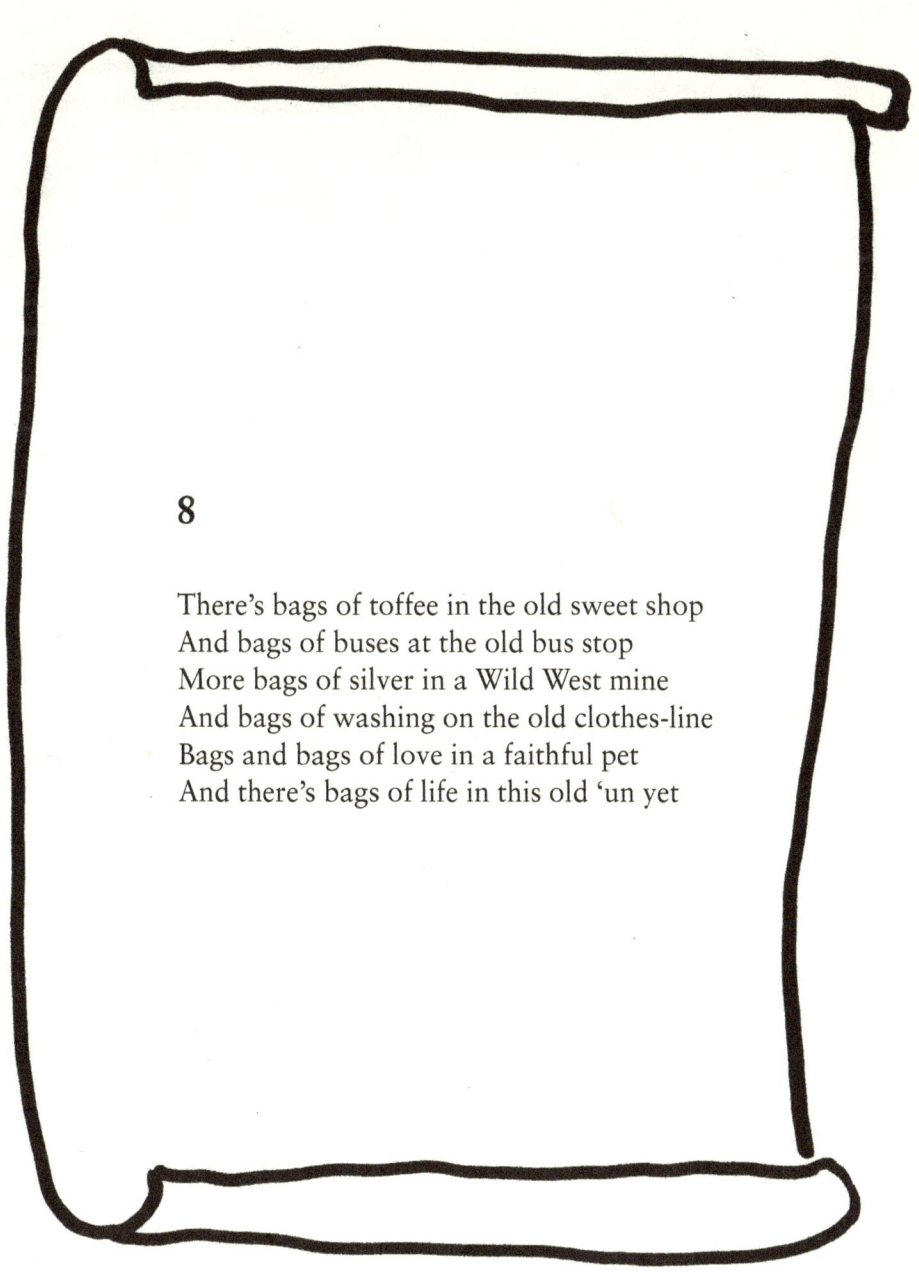

8

There's bags of toffee in the old sweet shop
And bags of buses at the old bus stop
More bags of silver in a Wild West mine
And bags of washing on the old clothes-line
Bags and bags of love in a faithful pet
And there's bags of life in this old 'un yet

9

I'm commissioned by senior management
To write some kind words about you
They suggested a tribute about your work
But had no real idea what you do

Boom Boom

So I tried to explain all your functions
And said you were one of the best
I said you did it five days out of seven
And could see they were very impressed

Boom Boom

I said it's not what you do that matters
But how you do it, sick or tired
They said that they couldn't agree with me more
Then they asked me to tell you, you're fired

Boom Boom

10

Who chronicled the path of man
As first he stumbled from the dark
I'll tell you who it was my friend
The planet Earth's first humble clerk

Claudius wrote about his life
He was 'The' Emperor of Rome
But it was with his quill in hand
That Claudius felt most at home

So you can see that anyone
Who dares to learn to write his name
No matter what his role in life
Is really in the `clerking game'

So when it's time to get the call
And to St Peter you must hark
When he enquires as to your trade
Just smile and say, like you, a clerk

11

One Arm Bandits

The coin drops and the tumblers fall
The other suckers hear the call
Mere drinkers only turn and glance
As suckers queue to take a chance

Another coin another spin
The suckers never ever win
Machines that pay increase the strain
For suckers have to play again

If just one wish were granted me
I'd wish these bandits in the sea
But gambling fever's in my brain
I'd no doubt fish them out again

The wise ones seem to know the way
They win one coin and walk away
I wish that I could do the same
But my cash goes straight down the drain

12

I wish that I could change the mess the world is in
Problems of religion and colour of the skin
But as my answers seem so crazy
And as I'm feeling very lazy
I'll just sit here picking the pimple on my chin

13

You can't stop the trickling sands of time
Or 12 inches from being a foot
Or the boss from thinking he's always right
Or your chimney from filling with soot

14

He swims shark-infested waters,
Fights gorillas hand to hand
And when walking on the seashore,
Leaves no footprint in the sand

He can climb the highest mountains,
Knows where natures' secrets stored
But told me only yesterday,
Deep inside he's really bored

15

I knew a lad with his clothes and music
That were influenced greatly by grunge
Who dived into a bone dry swimming pool
But landed safely on a damp sponge

16

<u>Don't wait up</u>

Don't waste your time waiting up for me
'Cos I think I'll be in with the milk

I've met somebody who says they care
They said they're taking me out somewhere
And if I get a present
And find it's something in silk, WELL

Don't waste your time waiting up for me
'Cos I think I'll be in with the milk

17

<u>Don't spit on the floor</u>

Don't ever spit on the floor my son
You must spit like your dad, down the sink

Spit on the floor makes my stomach turn
So make it one of the skills you learn
The way you void saliva
Says more of you than you think, SO

Don't ever spit on the floor my son
You must spit like your dad, down the sink

18

<u>Don't throw your bucket</u>

Don't throw your bucket down that there hole
It's the way into our septic tank

Around that hole no bird sings its song
And four million flies just can't be wrong
So cast your bone dry bucket
Down by the old riverbank, BUT

Don't throw your bucket down that there hole
It's the way into our septic tank

19

<u>Don't drink your bathwater</u>

Don't drink a drop of your bathwater son
There's four more to come after you

It was grandad who first discovered
That the water made quite a good brew
Quite a good aperitif
And truly wonderful stew, BUT

Don't drink a drop of your bathwater son
There's four more to come after you

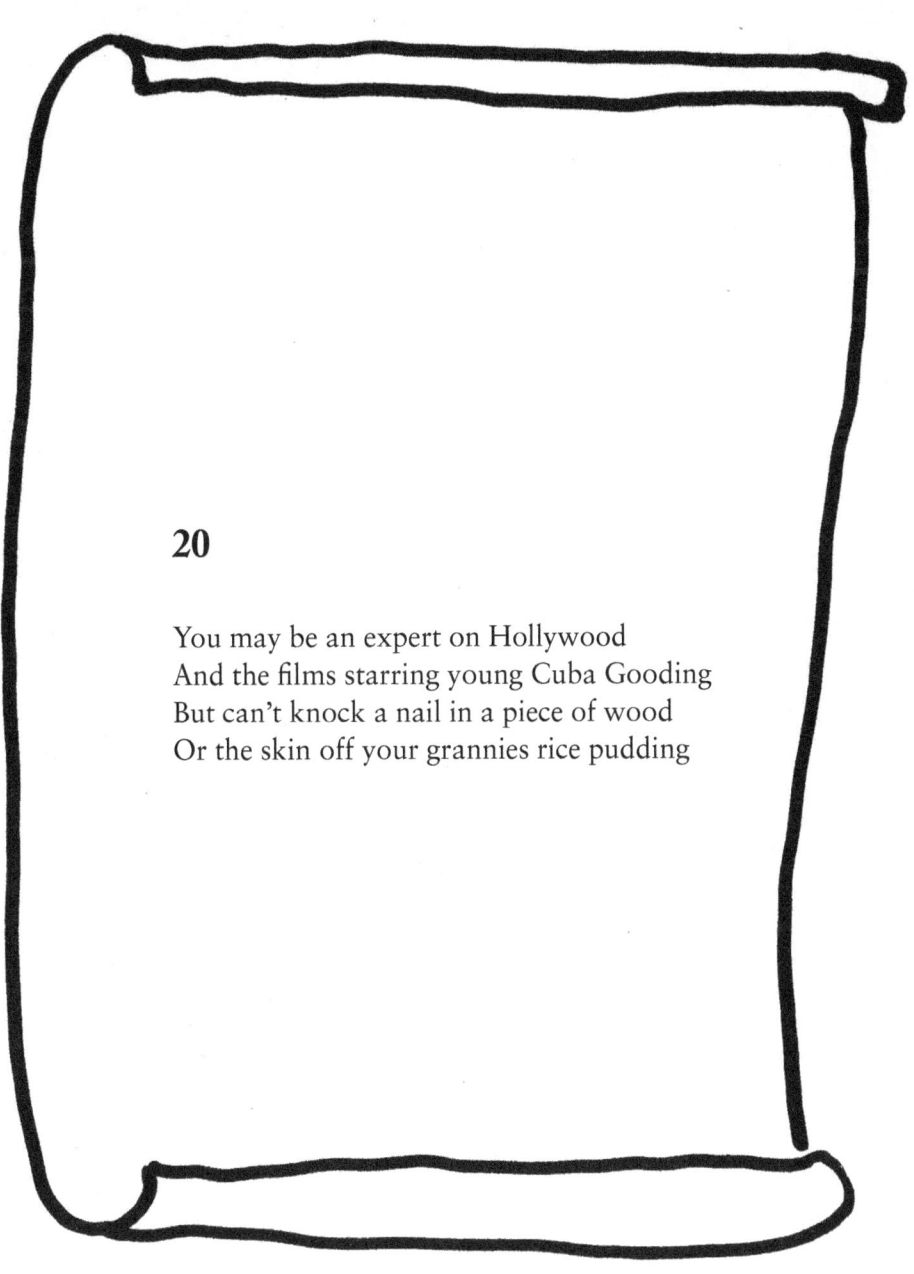

20

You may be an expert on Hollywood
And the films starring young Cuba Gooding
But can't knock a nail in a piece of wood
Or the skin off your grannies rice pudding

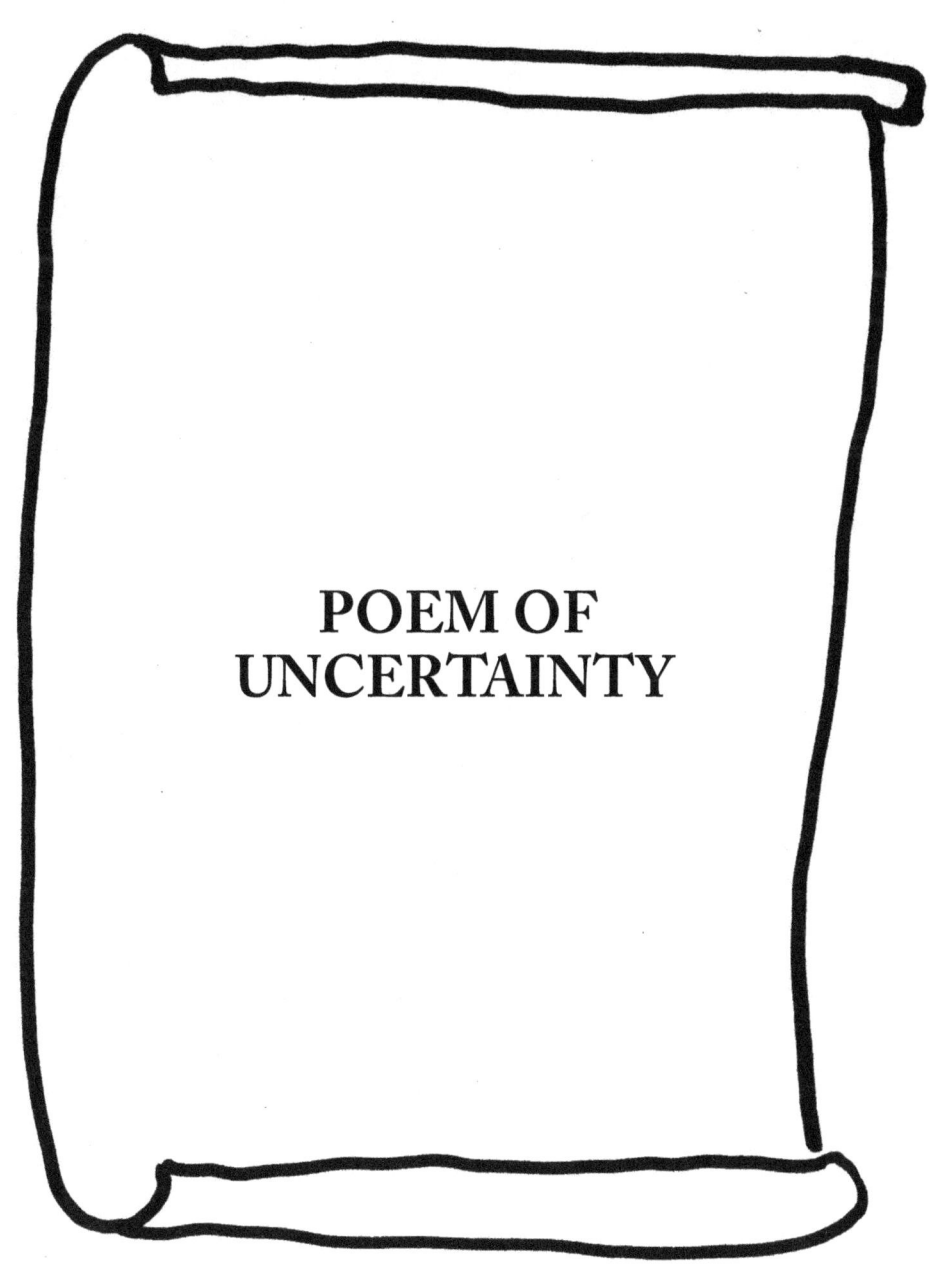

POEM OF UNCERTAINTY

I saw you on a boat, in a technicolour coat
But it was just a dream
The sun was in your hair, and you didn't have a care
But it was just a dream
And then you gave a smile, said you'd hug me in a while
But it was just a dream
Your face was very brave, as you gave a little wave
But it was just a dream
So very plain to see, you were sailing just for me
But it was just a dream

We always laughed as lovers do, and held each other tight
When you said that you had a dream, you'd go from me one night
You said although you had such love for me inside your heart
You'd only shed a single tear if we should ever part

A tree shook like a fan as the hurricane began
But was it just a dream
You shivered in the cold; said your bones would not grow old
But was it just a dream
The boat sank in the lake and the world began to shake
But was it just a dream
I woke up full of fear on my pillow just one tear
But was it just a dream
I looked across at you, you were looking at me too
And it was just a dream

THE BIG FINISH

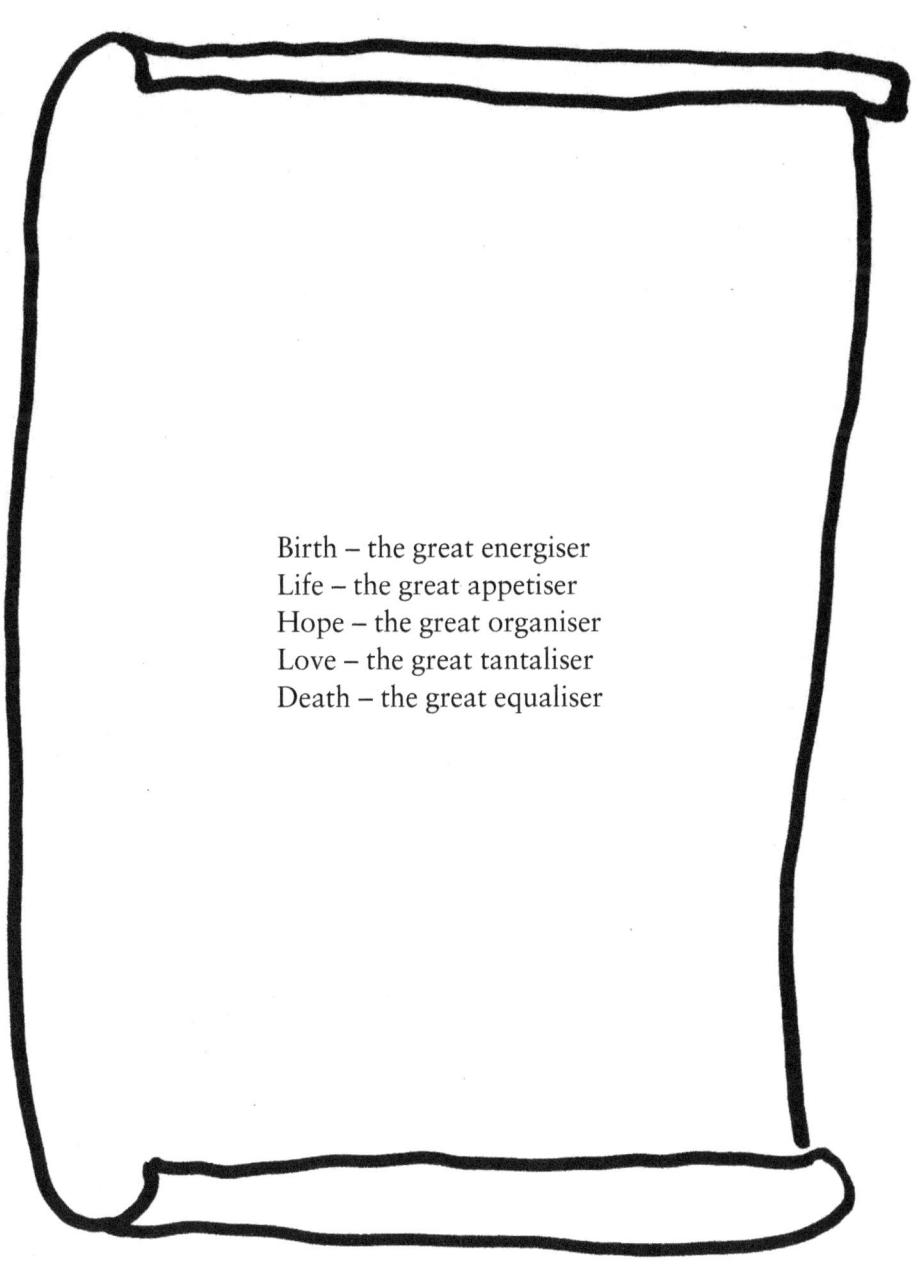

Birth – the great energiser
Life – the great appetiser
Hope – the great organiser
Love – the great tantaliser
Death – the great equaliser

www.ingramcontent.com/pod-product-compliance
Lightning Source LLC
Chambersburg PA
CBHW031408040426
42444CB00005B/467